Heavenly CHOCOLATE Recipes

Chocolate lovers are not known for their restraint. There are a few rare mortals who can confine themselves to one square of chocolate once a week, but the majority of us are so passionate about this irresistible ingredient that the idea of an entire cookbook devoted to it seems not only sensible but highly desirable. The book opens with information on the various types of chocolate and how to make the most of them. Cool and Creamy Desserts includes favourites like chocolate pots and chocolate mousse, and there's an entire chapter devoted to cheesecakes and pies. Remember that wonderful sponge pudding whose top concealed a creamy chocolate sauce? You'll find the recipe in the chapter on hot puddings and pancakes, along with a classic chocolate soufflé and a fabulous fondue. As for cakes, all feature – great and small – from internationally known Devil's Food Cake and Black Forest Gâteau to family favourites like chocolate fudge cake and marble cake. And with simple recipes for chocolate chip cookies and crunchies, the biscuit barrel need never be empty again. Finally, if you can bear to share, there's a chapter devoted to fudge, truffles and other edible gifts.

CONTENTS

CHOCOLATE KNOW-HOW

Few ingredients are as versatile as chocolate. It lends its incomparable flavour to confectionery, cakes, biscuits, puddings, sauces and drinks, and can even be added to savoury dishes. A square of dark chocolate, stirred into a robust meat casserole will boost the flavour, especially when tomatoes and chillies are present, at the same time giving the sauce a rich gloss.

Ever since the Aztecs raised their brimming cups of chocolate, this mysterious ingredient has given pleasure to people the world over. When it was initially introduced to Europe it met with huge success, and it was not long before all the most fashionable resorts and cities boasted cocoa houses. When sugar was added to the beverage it became even more popular, and when, some two centuries later, eating chocolate was produced in bars, the boom really got under way.

Chocolate and cocoa both come from the cacao tree, which grows in South and Central America, the West Indies and parts of Malaysia and West Africa. The fruit is a large pod which grows on the trunk and main branches of the tree. It is harvested twice a year and the pods split to reveal the cocoa beans. After fermentation the beans are shelled and the kernels or nibs dried and roasted to intensify the flavour.

Pressing yields a thick liquor which contains about fifty percent fat (cocoa butter). If the liquor is partially defatted and cooled it solidifies to a block. This is bitter chocolate.

More often, however, the liquor is enriched with extra cocoa butter, then blended and stirred to give it its characteristic creaminess. Milk may be added and the chocolate may be sweetened.

The higher the percentage of cocoa solids the better. For good results in cooking, look for a chocolate with at least 50 percent.

When most of the cocoa fat has been extracted from the liquor, what remains is a solid chocolate block. This is powdered to make cocoa.

Drinking chocolate is a relatively new product. It has a high sugar content, and has been treated so that it dissolves readily in hot or cold water.

TYPES OF CHOCOLATE

Couverture: The quality of cooking chocolate can vary widely. Professionals plump for couverture, which is pure chocolate with no fats other than cocoa butter. The best dark couverture may consist of as much as 70 percent cocoa solids, with an intense flavour. However, couverture may need to be treated before use in order to distribute the cocoa fat evenly. The process (tempering) involves pouring the melted chocolate onto a marble slab and then lifting and folding it until it is shiny and smooth. Specialist chocolate shops sell tempered chocolate.

Bakers' Chocolate: This is a compound, with other fats replacing some of the cocoa butter to give a product which melts readily and is easy to use.

Plain Chocolate: The chocolate used most frequently for cooking, however, is the common or garden confectionery labelled plain chocolate and sold at supermarkets, corner shops and sweetshops. In recent years the quality of plain chocolate has improved greatly, with many of the bars boasting at least 50 percent cocoa solids. The amount of sugar varies. Experiment to find the chocolate that suits you best; the supermarket's own brand may well prove ideal for everyday cooking, although you may prefer to use couverture for confectionery and glazes.

Milk Chocolate: This contains powdered or condensed milk. It is the most popular chocolate for eating, but is not as suitable for cooking as it separates quickly on heating. It is used for decoration.

White Chocolate: A sweet, waxy product, white chocolate contains cocoa butter but no chocolate liquor. It is useful for providing a colour contrast but has very little flavour.

The pictures on these pages show some of chocolate's many forms, from cocoa beans, flaked solid cocoa, couverture and vermicelli (right) to grated chocolate and caraque (left). The larger photograph also shows Hot Chocolate (page 46), Chocolate-coated Hazelnuts (page 45), Chocolate Nut Pie (page 14).

STORING CHOCOLATE

Unopened bars and packets of chocolate should keep for at least 6 months in a cool dry place. Wrap any opened bars carefully as they can absorb other flavours. A whitish bloom sometimes appears on chocolate; this is merely cocoa fat coming to the surface and will not affect the flavour.

MELTING CHOCOLATE

Chocolate burns very easily and must always be melted slowly, over gentle heat. One of the best ways to do this is to break the chocolate into squares and put it in a heat-proof bowl. Bring a small saucepan of water to the boil, then remove it from the heat and place the bowl on top. Leave the chocolate until it has melted before stirring it.

Chocolate is sometimes melted in a pan with other ingredients such as milk, cream, butter or coffee. Follow instructions in individual recipes. White chocolate is usually melted with a little fresh or soured cream.

Chocolate may be melted in a bowl in the microwave, but it is essential to use a low setting. The squares of chocolate will retain their shape, so don't rely on a visual test for melting. Keep the timing short and test frequently with a cocktail stick.

When melting chocolate over hot water, take care that droplets of moisture do not come into contact with the chocolate, or it will stiffen and clog. Beating in a little cream may rescue it, but this cannot be guaranteed.

COVERING A CAKE

Melted chocolate makes a glossy cake covering. Fill the cake, if liked, and place it on a serving plate. Brush off any surface crumbs. Melt 250g (8oz) plain chocolate over hot water, stir it lightly, then carefully pour it over the cake. Using a palette knife, swiftly spread the chocolate evenly over the top and sides of the cake. As the chocolate cools, the surface may be swirled with a clean palette knife.

PIPING CHOCOLATE

Melted chocolate can be tricky to pipe. Practise on greaseproof paper first, or use chocolate buttercream until you become proficient. Some of the easier designs are illustrated left: Stars are made by using a paper piping bag fitted with a star nozzle. Hold the bag at right angles and apply even pressure to make a round, then stop applying pressure and lift the bag to finish the star. To make shells, hold the bag at an angle of 45°, varying the pressure. For dots, snailtrails and squiggles, use melted chocolate in a bag fitted with a writing nozzle.

RUNOUTS

Chocolate runouts can be made in almost any shape. Trace a simple design on wax paper; tape it to a flat surface. Place a little melted chocolate in a paper bag fitted with a writing nozzle. Pipe outlines, keeping joins neat. Fit a clean writing nozzle in a fresh paper bag and fill in the centres, either making solid designs or producing a lacy effect. If necessary, use a wooden toothpick or cocktail stick to ease chocolate into corners. Leave runouts to set, then carefully pull paper away from them.

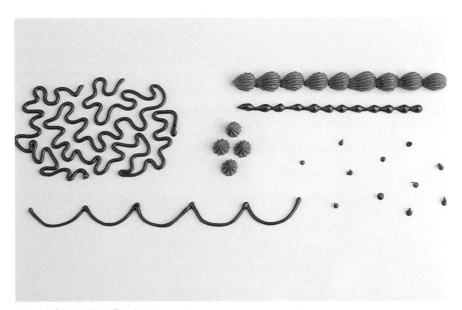

Piped Chocolate Designs

Chocolate Runouts

CHOCOLATE CARAQUE AND CURLS

Illustrated on page 2

To make caraque, melt 250g (8oz) plain chocolate and pour it onto a clean smooth surface such as a marble slab. Leave until set. Holding a long knife with a rigid blade at an angle of about 45° to the chocolate, draw it lightly across to cut thin layers that curl into scrolls. For fans, use the tip of a round-bladed knife.

Curls are very easy to make using a potato peeler. The chocolate should not be too cold or it will break.

CHOCOLATE LEAVES

This simple decoration is highly effective. Any non-poisonous leaves may be used; rose leaves work particularly well. Wipe the leaves clean, dry them, then, using a small paintbrush, thickly coat the underside of each with melted chocolate. Allow to set on wax paper, chocolate side up, then carefully peel away the leaves.

DIPPING CHOCOLATE

Truffles, nuts and fresh or crystallized fruits taste delicious when wholly or partially dipped in melted chocolate. Hold the fruit by the stalk or use a cocktail stick. Allow the excess chocolate to drip back into the bowl, then transfer to a baking sheet lined with nonstick baking parchment. Serve on the day of dipping. Dip nuts one at a time or in clusters (see page 45). Nuts, crystallised fruit and truffles may be dipped ahead of time.

CHOCOLATE CASES

Use paper sweet cases as moulds for shaping chocolate cases. To coat about 20 cases you will need 125g (4oz) plain or white chocolate. Melt the chocolate, then use a teaspoon to coat the inside of each paper case, keeping the coating level and scooping out any excess. Invert the cases and chill to set. Peel away paper and fill cases with chocolate mousse, piped Ganache (page 11) or whipped cream. For more ideas, see Cherry Dreams (page 42) and Ginger Twirls (page 44).

Chocolate Leaves

Dipping chocolate

Chocolate Cases

COOL AND CREAMY DESSERTS

Dip into a dreamy chocolate mousse, dark and delectable, or try the cool contrast of a hazelnut and chocolate chip ice cream served in an individual meringue basket. Whether you want something special for the family or a spectacular new party piece, look no further. The answer is right here.

Partial Eclipse

175g (6oz) dark chocolate, broken into squares

300ml (10fl oz) double cream

2 tspn powdered gelatine

4 tblspn water

3 egg yolks

4 tblspn caster sugar

155ml (5fl oz) crème fraîche

White Chocolate Mousse

200g (6¹/₂oz) white chocolate

4 tblspn milk

2 tspn powdered gelatine

4 tblspn water

3 egg yolks

4 tblspn caster sugar

155ml (5fl oz) double cream

155ml (5fl oz) Greek yogurt

To Serve

375ml (12fl oz) single cream

60g (2oz) dark chocolate

1 Melt dark chocolate with 2 tablespoons of the double cream (see page 4).

2 Meanwhile sprinkle gelatine on top of measured water in a cup. When spongy, melt over hot water. Combine egg yolks and caster sugar in a bowl. Whisk until pale and thick, then, using a spatula, fold the egg mixture into the melted chocolate until thoroughly combined.

3 Mix 1 tablespoon of the chocolate mixture with the gelatine, then stir gelatine into bowl, mixing thoroughly. Set bowl aside in a cool place until mixture starts to thicken.

4 Whip remaining double cream with crème fraîche until soft peaks form; fold into dark chocolate mixture and chill until mixture is firm enough to hold its shape when spooned.

5 Meanwhile make white chocolate mousse. Melt chocolate with milk (see page 4). Dissolve gelatine in measured water, then melt over hot water. Whisk egg yolks with sugar until pale and thick. Using a spatula, fold the egg mixture into the melted white chocolate mixture. Mix 1 tablespoon of mixture with gelatine, then stir gelatine into remaining white chocolate mixture.

6 Whip cream with yogurt until soft peaks form; fold into white chocolate mixture. Chill until mixture is firm enough to hold its shape when spooned.

7 Brush 8 ramekins or custard cups lightly with oil. Spoon dark chocolate mousse into the left half of each ramekin, smoothing it neatly down the centre, then fill the right halves with white chocolate mousse, taking care that the two do not mix. Chill the mousses until firm, about 3 hours.

8 Carefully run a knife around the inside of each ramekin or custard cup and invert the mousses on dessert plates. Surround each mousse with a small puddle of single cream. Melt the dark chocolate in a small jug and drip dots of chocolate into the custard at regular intervals around each mousse. Drag a toothpick through the dots to form hearts. Serve.

Serves 8

Quick Chocolate Mousses

3 eggs, separated

2 tblspn caster sugar

125g (4oz) plain chocolate

pinch salt

whipped cream and chocolate caraque (page 5) to decorate

1 In a large bowl, whisk egg yolks with caster sugar until mixture is pale and creamy and beaters leave a trail when lifted.

2 Melt chocolate (page 4). As soon as it is soft, whisk it into egg yolk mixture until smoothly combined.

3 Whisk egg whites with salt in a clean dry bowl until stiff. Beat a little of the egg white into the chocolate mixture to lighten it, then fold in the rest.

4 Divide mixture between 4-6 small dishes or glasses; chill for 2 hours or until set. Decorate with whipped cream and chocolate caraque.

Serves 4-6

Variations
Rum, brandy, orange liqueur, coffee essence or finely chopped nuts may be used to flavour the mousse. Fold the chosen flavouring in with the stiffly beaten egg whites.

Chocolate Trifle

1 packet chocolate blancmange powder

3 tblspn sugar, plus extra for sprinkling

600ml (1 pt) milk

1 egg yolk

2 x 250g (8oz) chocolate Swiss rolls with jam or buttercream filling

1 x 350g (11oz) can mandarin orange segments, drained

300ml (10fl oz) double cream

chocolate vermicelli to decorate

1 Combine blancmange powder and sugar in a bowl. Stir in 2 tablespoons of the milk to make a smooth paste. Warm remaining milk in a saucepan; pour onto blancmange mixture, stirring well. Return mixture to pan. Heat, stirring constantly until mixture boils, then lower heat and simmer for 1 minute, continuing to stir. Remove from heat, cool slightly, then beat in egg yolk. Pour into a bowl, sprinkle surface with a little sugar to prevent the formation of a skin, and set aside to cool.

2 Cut Swiss rolls into 5cm (2in) slices; line base and sides of a 1 litre (1³/₄pt) glass bowl, cutting slices in half if necessary to fill gaps and create an attractive design.

3 Drain mandarins, reserving the syrup. Sprinkle syrup over Swiss roll slices to moisten, then scatter mandarin segments over base of lined bowl.

4 Pour cold blancmange into bowl. Whisk cream until it stands in peaks, then carefully spread in an even layer over chocolate blancmange. Swirl with a knife. Chill for 1 hour before serving, decorated with chocolate vermicelli.

Serves 6

Kitchen Tip

If you do not have any chocolate blancmange powder, make 600ml (1pt) chocolate custard, mixing about 2 tablespoons cocoa with the custard powder.

Mocha Mousses

1 tblspn instant coffee powder

2 tblspn boiling water

75g (2¹/₂oz) plain chocolate, broken into squares

1 tspn coffee liqueur (optional)

3 eggs, separated

60g (2oz) caster sugar

155ml (5fl oz) whipping cream, whipped

grated chocolate to decorate

1 Dissolve coffee powder in boiling water in a heatproof bowl. Add chocolate, with liqueur (if using) and melt over hot water (see page 4), stirring occasionally.

2 Whisk egg yolks and sugar in a bowl until thick and creamy. Gradually whisk in all the melted chocolate mixture.

3 In separate bowls, whip cream until soft peaks form; whisk egg whites until stiff. Fold cream into mocha mixture, then egg whites. Divide mixture between 6 ramekins. Chill for 3-4 hours or until set. Decorate with grated chocolate.

Serves 6

Chocolate Trifle

Iced Chocolate Boxes

Little Pots of Chocolate

500g (1lb) dark chocolate, broken into squares

finely grated rind of 1 orange

juice of 3 oranges

60g (2oz) butter

2 tblspn Grand Marnier or other orange liqueur

2 eggs, separated, plus 2 egg yolks

Decoration

2 orange slices

4 tspn orange liqueur as chosen for chocolate pots

1 Melt chocolate with orange rind, juice and butter in a heavy-based saucepan over very low heat. Stir occasionally. As soon as chocolate has melted and mixture is smooth, remove from the heat and stir in the Grand Marnier or other orange liqueur.

2 Whisk egg yolks in a large mixing bowl until pale and creamy. Using a fine sieve, strain in chocolate mixture, whisking constantly if possible. Alternatively, whisk mixture thoroughly after adding chocolate.

3 Whisk egg whites in clean dry bowl until stiff but not dry; fold into chocolate mixture.

4 Divide mixture between four 155ml (5fl oz) glass or china cups or dishes; chill for 2 hours or until set.

5 Just before serving, cut each orange slice into quarters. Carefully pour 1 teaspoon of the chosen orange liqueur over the top of each little pot of chocolate, gently rotating the cup or glass until the surface is coated. Decorate each portion with 2 pieces of sliced orange and serve at once, with dessert biscuits, if liked.

Serves 4

Iced Chocolate Boxes

1 x 500ml (16fl oz) block chocolate ice cream

24 square peppermint cream chocolates

155ml (5fl oz) double cream

icing sugar (optional)

1 x 375g (12oz) can mandarin orange segments, drained

6 small mint sprigs to decorate

1 Cut ice cream block into six equal cubes, using one of the peppermint chocolates as a guide. The sides of each cube should measure the same as the chocolate.

2 Press one chocolate onto each side of each ice cream cube, boxing it in as illustrated above. Arrange the iced chocolate boxes on a platter or individual plates; place in the freezer until required.

3 Whip cream until thick but not stiff, sweetening with a little icing sugar if liked. Place in a piping bag fitted with a large star nozzle.

4 Remove chocolate boxes from freezer. Pipe a generous swirl of cream on top of each box. Decorate with mandarin orange segments and mint sprigs. Serve immediately, before ice cream melts.

Serves 6

Chocolate Hazelnut Meringue Baskets

Chocolate Hazelnut Meringue Baskets

4 egg whites

pinch salt

280g (9oz) icing sugar

Ice Cream

125g (4oz) caster sugar

300ml (10fl oz) milk

600ml (1pt) double cream

8 egg yolks

155g (5oz) ground hazelnuts

60g (2oz) toasted hazelnuts, chopped

90g (3oz) chocolate chips

Chocolate Sauce

185g (6oz) plain chocolate

60g (2oz) butter

185ml (6fl oz) double cream

vanilla essence (optional)

1 Preheat oven to 150°C (300°F/ Gas 2). Cut 2 pieces of nonstick baking parchment to fit two baking sheets. Invert the baking parchment and draw four circles on each piece, each measuring 7.5cm (3in) in diameter. Replace the parchment, pencilled side down.

2 In a large heatproof bowl, whisk egg whites with salt until stiff. Whisk in icing sugar, 1 tablespoon at a time. Place the bowl over a saucepan of gently simmering water; continue to whisk for about 5 minutes until meringue is stiff.

3 Spoon meringue into a piping bag fitted with a fluted nozzle and, starting in the centre of each circle, pipe 6 individual meringue baskets, using a spiral action and making the sides three spirals high.

4 Bake meringue baskets for 1¼-1½ hours. Cool on a wire rack, then store in an airtight tin.

5 Make ice cream. Combine sugar, milk and cream in a saucepan. Bring to the boil, stirring to dissolve the sugar. Remove from the heat. In a bowl, beat egg yolks lightly. Add scalded cream mixture in a thin stream, beating constantly to make a light foamy mixture. Transfer to the top of a double boiler (or a heatproof bowl) and place over simmering water. Stir until custard coats the back of a spoon, then pour into a clean bowl and chill in a larger bowl filled with ice. As soon as custard is cool, cover it closely and refrigerate for 2 hours.

6 Fold in ground hazelnuts. Pour into an ice cream maker and chill according to instructions, adding the chopped nuts and chocolate chips when churning is almost complete. Alternatively, freeze in ice trays. When semi-frozen, beat mixture to break up any large ice crystals. Repeat the process twice more, adding the chopped hazelnuts and chocolate chips during the final beating. Freeze in a suitable container until ice cream is solid.

7 About 30 minutes before serving, transfer the ice cream to the refrigerator to soften slightly. Make the chocolate sauce. Melt chocolate with butter in a heavy-based saucepan. Gradually beat in cream and warm through, stirring constantly.

8 Arrange the meringue baskets on individual plates. Place 2 scoops of ice cream in each basket, then top each scoop of ice cream with hot chocolate sauce. Serve at once.

Serves 6

Kitchen Tips
For a quick cheat's pudding use a good quality bought ice cream (coffee is delicious). Don't be tempted to use bought meringue baskets, however, unless you have access to a good baker. The super-sweet, dry meringues sold in packs in supermarkets are not suitable. Make a plain vanilla ice cream by omitting the hazelnuts and adding 2 teaspoons natural vanilla essence. Before scooping it into the meringue baskets, fill them with strawberrries or raspberries for a summer treat.

Black Bottom Sundaes

6 scoops good quality chocolate ice cream
6 scoops good quality vanilla ice cream
6 tspn Tia Maria liqueur (optional)
Ganache
220g (7oz) dark chocolate, broken into squares
155ml (5fl oz) double cream
Decoration
4 marrons glacés
25g (1oz) slivered almonds, toasted

1 Start by making the ganache. Melt chocolate (see page 4). Heat cream in a heavy-based saucepan. As soon as cream approaches boiling point, remove the pan from the heat and add the cream in a slow steady stream to the melted chocolate, whisking constantly with a balloon whisk until mixture is completely smooth. Cool, whisking occasionally, then chill until ganache is cold and thick.

2 About 30 minutes before serving the sundaes, transfer both ice creams to the refrigerator to soften. Using a hand-held electric mixer, whip the ganache until it holds its shape; the colour will lighten slightly.

3 Place a scoop of chocolate ice cream in each of six tall sundae glasses. If using the liqueur, drizzle 1 teaspoon over each portion of chocolate ice cream. Top with vanilla ice cream.

4 Spoon or pipe a generous amount of ganache on top of each sundae, swirling it in the centre. Decorate with the marrons glacés and toasted almonds. Serve at once.

Serves 6

Black Bottom Sundaes

Italian Chestnut Chocolate Bombe

900ml (1½pt) good quality chocolate ice cream

250g (8oz) drained canned whole chestnuts in syrup

250g (8oz) sweetened chestnut purée

1-2 tblspn brandy

375ml (12fl oz) double cream

1 egg white

Decoration

whipped cream

glacé cherries

marrons glacés

holly leaves or chocolate leaves (page 5)

1 About 1 hour before you plan to start making the bombe, chill a 1.8 litre (3pt) bombe mould in the freezer. At the same time, transfer chocolate ice cream to the refrigerator to soften.

2 Spoon ice cream into the chilled mould, smoothing it over the bottom and up the sides to make a shell about 2cm (¾in) thick. Cover and freeze until firm.

3 Roughly chop drained chestnuts. Spoon them into the lined mould, pressing them gently into the ice cream over the bottom and sides. Cover and freeze again.

4 Whisk chestnut purée with brandy in a bowl until well combined. In a separate bowl, whip cream until soft peaks form. Fold into chestnut purée.

5 In a clean dry bowl, whisk egg white until stiff; fold gently into chestnut mixture. Spoon into the centre of the bombe, cover again and freeze until solid.

6 About 30 minutes before serving, turn out bombe onto a flat serving dish. Transfer the bombe to the refrigerator to soften slightly.

7 Just before serving, decorate with piped whipped cream, glacé cherries, sliced marrons glacés and holly or chocolate leaves.

Serves 12

Profiteroles

75g (2½oz) strong white flour (bread flour)

60g (2oz) butter

155ml (5fl oz) water

2 eggs, beaten

Filling and Topping

250ml (8fl oz) whipping cream

1 tblspn icing sugar

2-3 drops vanilla essence

hot Chocolate Sauce (see Chocolate Hazelnut Meringue Baskets on page 10)

1 Preheat oven to 220°C (425°F/ Gas 7). Lightly grease 2 baking sheets. Make choux pastry for profiteroles. Sift flour onto a piece of greaseproof paper. Melt butter over low heat in a large saucepan. Add water and bring to the boil. Add flour all at once, and beat mixture vigorously until it leaves sides of pan. Remove pan from heat and cool slightly, then beat in eggs, about 1 tablespoon at a time.

2 Spoon mixture into a piping bag fitted with a plain nozzle. Pipe 2cm (¾in) balls onto baking sheets. Bake for 10 minutes, reduce temperature to 180°C (350°F/Gas 4) and bake for 20-25 minutes. Cut a slit in each bun. Cool on wire racks.

3 For filling, whip cream with icing sugar and vanilla essence. Fill choux buns. Pile the buns on a serving dish and pour over the hot chocolate sauce. Serve at once.

Serves 4-6

Kitchen Tip
It is not essential to use strong flour, but it does give a better result.

Chocolate Charlotte

1 packet of 8 trifle sponges

375ml (12fl oz) milk

185g (6oz) caster sugar

3 egg yolks

15g (½oz) powdered gelatine

4 tblspn water

90g (3oz) dark or bitter chocolate

90ml (3fl oz) brandy or liqueur

500ml (16fl oz) double cream

whipped cream to decorate

1 Slice trifle sponges in half horizontally. Brush a 1.5 litre (2½pt) charlotte mould with oil, line with clingfilm and brush again with oil. Cover base of mould with sponges, cutting as necessary to fit. Line mould with remaining sponges, making sure all gaps are filled. Reserve sponge trimmings.

2 Heat milk in a large saucepan. Stir in 90g (3oz) of the sugar until dissolved. Bring to just below boiling point; set aside.

3 Whisk egg yolks and remaining sugar in a bowl until mixture is pale and creamy and beaters leave a trail when lifted. Pour in hot milk in a steady stream, stirring, then place mixture in a heatproof bowl over simmering water. Cook, stirring constantly, until custard coats the back of a spoon. Strain custard into a bowl and set aside to cool, beating occasionally.

4 Sprinkle gelatine onto cold water in a small bowl. When spongy, melt over hot water. Cool slightly, then stir into custard.

5 Melt chocolate with brandy or liqueur (see page 4), cool slightly, then stir into custard mixture. Place the bowl in a bowl of ice and stir until on the point of setting.

6 Whip cream to soft peaks; fold into custard. Pour into prepared charlotte mould and chill overnight.

7 About 10 minutes before serving, unmould charlotte. Trim ragged pieces of sponge, remove the clingfilm and decorate the base with rosettes of whipped cream.

Serves 8

Kitchen Tip
If joins are visible in sponge on top of the charlotte, crumb reserved sponge trimmings and sprinkle the crumbs lightly over the top. A 20cm (8in) sponge cake can be used instead of trifle sponges.

Chocolate Charlotte

CHEESECAKES, PIES AND TERRINES

Ever since the sixties, when the cheesecake topped the pudding popularity poll, this simply delicious combination of crisp crumb or pastry case and creamy light filling has been unbeatable. Today's cheesecakes, pies and terrines explore new flavour combinations, with chocolate a key ingredient.

Dreamy Chocolate Cheesecake

155g (5oz) butter

1 x 315g (10oz) packet bourbon biscuits (12 biscuits), finely crushed

Filling

250g (8oz) ricotta cheese

250g (8oz) full fat soft cheese

60g (2oz) caster sugar

grated rind and juice of 1/2 lemon

1/4 tspn vanilla essence

300ml (10fl oz) single cream

1 tblspn powdered gelatine

3 tblspn water

90g (3oz) plain chocolate, broken into squares

drained canned mandarin orange segments to decorate

1 Lightly oil a 20cm (8in) spring-form cake tin. Melt butter in a small pan, stir in biscuit crumbs and mix well. Press over base and sides of the prepared tin, cover and chill for 30 minutes until firm.

2 To make the filling, beat ricotta and soft cheese in a large bowl until well combined. Beat in sugar, lemon rind and juice, vanilla essence and cream; mix well.

3 Sprinkle gelatine onto cold water in a small bowl. When spongy, melt over hot water. Cool slightly, then gradually stir into cheese mixture. Pour filling into chilled biscuit shell. Level surface.

4 Melt chocolate (see page 4). Pour over cheesecake filling.

Using a skewer, swirl chocolate through filling to give a marble effect. Cover the tin carefully and chill for 3 hours or until set.

5 To serve, run a knife around edge of cheesecake, carefully remove sides of tin and slide cake onto a serving plate. Decorate with mandarin orange segments.

Serves 6-8

Chocolate Nut Pie

Illustrated on page 3

1 x 215g (7 1/2oz) packet frozen shortcrust pastry, thawed

90g (3oz) butter

125g (4oz) sugar

125g (4oz) plain flour

2 eggs

90g (3oz) pecans or walnuts, coarsely chopped

155g (5oz) plain chocolate, grated

1 Preheat oven to 180°C (350°F/ Gas 4). Roll out pastry and line a 20cm (8in) pie plate.

2 Melt butter in a saucepan. Off the heat, stir in sugar and flour; beat until smooth. Add eggs and mix well. Finally stir in nuts and chocolate until well combined.

3 Spoon the filling into the pastry case. Bake for 30 minutes. Serve warm, with whipped or clotted cream, or cold, decorated with whipped cream and chocolate caraque (page 5).

Serves 4

Dreamy Chocolate Cheesecake

White Chocolate Cheesecake with Strawberry Topping

220g (7oz) golden oatmeal biscuits

60g (2oz) butter

Filling

4 tspn powdered gelatine

4 tblspn water

155g (5oz) white chocolate, broken into squares

155ml (5fl oz) soured cream

125g (4oz) cream cheese

250g (8oz) ricotta cheese

grated rind and juice of 1 orange

90g (3oz) caster sugar

Topping

250g (8oz) strawberries, hulled

4 tblspn redcurrant jelly

1 tblspn lemon juice

1 Lightly oil a 23cm (9in) spring form cake tin. Crumb biscuits in a food processor or place them in a stout polythene bag and crush with a rolling pin. Melt butter in a small pan, stir in biscuit crumbs and mix well. Press onto the base of the prepared tin, cover and chill until firm.

2 Make filling. Sprinkle gelatine on top of measured water in a cup. When spongy, melt over hot water. Cool slightly. Combine white chocolate and soured cream in a heatproof bowl. Set over gently simmering water until chocolate melts into cream. Stir until smooth.

3 Place cream cheese, ricotta, orange rind, orange juice and sugar in a blender or food processor. Process until thoroughly combined. Then, with the motor running, pour in the melted white chocolate mixture through the feeder tube.

4 Stir about 2 tablespoons of the cream cheese mixture into the melted gelatine, then replace the lid on the blender or food processor, turn the machine on and add the gelatine mixture through the feeder tube; process briefly to combine.

5 Pour the filling onto the chilled biscuit base and return the cheesecake to the refrigerator for 3-4 hours until set.

6 For topping, slice strawberries lengthwise and arrange them in concentric circles on the set cheesecake. In a small saucepan, heat redcurrant jelly with lemon juice until melted. Spoon over strawberries, coating them completely. When topping is cool, chill cheesecake for 1-2 hours more before serving.

Serves 6-8

Mocha Chiffon Flan

1 tblspn powdered gelatine

3 tblspn water

375ml (12fl oz) milk

2 tblspn instant coffee powder

3 eggs, separated

90g (3oz) caster sugar

2 tblspn chocolate liqueur or brandy

155ml (5fl oz) double cream, whipped

125g (4oz) chocolate caraque (page 5) to decorate

Pastry

250g (8oz) plain flour

pinch salt

125g (4oz) cold butter, cubed

60g (2oz) caster sugar

1 egg yolk

1 Preheat oven to 200°C (400°F/ Gas 6). Make pastry. Mix flour and salt in a bowl. Rub in butter, then stir in sugar. Add egg yolk with enough iced water to make a firm dough; chill for 30 minutes.

2 Roll out pastry and line a 23cm (9in) flan tin. Line with grease proof paper, add baking beans and bake blind for 7 minutes. Remove paper and beans. Bake pie shell for 10-15 minutes more, until golden. Seat aside to cool.

3 Sprinkle gelatine on top of measured water in a cup. When spongy, melt over hot water.

4 Heat milk and coffee powder to simmering point. In the top of a double boiler, whisk egg yolks with half the sugar until fluffy. Gradually whisk in flavoured milk, then stir over simmering water until custard coats the back of a spoon. Cool

Mocha Chiffon Flan

Sicilian Chocolate Cream Pie

slightly, then whisk in dissolved gelatine. Transfer to a bowl; cool over ice, stirring until mixture starts to thicken.

5 Stir in liqueur or brandy; fold in whipped cream. Whisk egg whites until stiff; gradually adding remaining sugar. Fold into mocha mixture, then pour into pastry case. Chill until set. Decorate flan with chocolate caraque.

Serves 6

Mint Chocolate Cheesecake

250g (8oz) digestive biscuits, crushed

90g (3oz) melted butter

1 tblspn powdered gelatine

3 tblspn water

220g (7oz) cream cheese

155g (5oz) ricotta cheese

125ml (4fl oz) soured cream

200g (7oz) dark chocolate, melted (page 4)

2 Peppermint Aero bars, crushed

250ml (8fl oz) double cream

whipped cream and grated chocolate to decorate

1 Combine biscuit crumbs and melted butter; press over base and sides of a 23cm (9in) flan tin. Chill until firm.

2 Sprinkle gelatine on top of measured water in a cup. When spongy, melt over hot water. Set aside to cool slightly.

3 Blend or process cream cheese with ricotta and soured cream until smooth. With motor running, add melted chocolate gradually through feeder tube, then add dissolved gelatine in the same way. Scrape into a bowl and stir in crushed peppermint chocolate. Whip cream and fold in.

4 Pour into flan shell; chill until firm. Decorate with whipped cream and grated chocolate.

Serves 12

Kitchen Tip
A 100g (3¹/₂oz) bar of peppermint crisp chocolate may be used instead of the Aeros. Grate the chocolate and add it with whipped cream. If you prefer a more pronounced peppermint flavour, add a little peppermint essence.

Sicilian Chocolate Cream Pie

500g (1lb) ricotta cheese

3 tblspn orange liqueur

90g (3oz) caster sugar

60g (2oz) bitter chocolate, grated

60g (2oz) candied orange peel, finely chopped, plus extra for topping

2 tblspn smooth apricot jam

23cm (9in) baked pastry case (see Mocha Chiffon Flan opposite)

grated chocolate to decorate

1 Beat ricotta in a bowl until creamy, then stir in liqueur, sugar, chocolate and orange peel. Chill the mixture for 1 hour to allow flavours to blend.

2 Heat jam until liquid; brush over inside of pastry case. Fill with cheese mixture and chill until required. Just before serving, sprinkle the cream pie with grated chocolate and the extra peel.

Serves 6-8

Iced White Chocolate Slice

Iced White Chocolate Slice

185g (6oz) white chocolate, broken into pieces

155ml (5fl oz) single cream

300ml (10fl oz) double cream

2 tblspn Amaretto (almond liqueur)

125g (4oz) ratafia or almond biscuits, crushed

icing sugar

Apricot Sauce

1 x 440g (14oz) can apricot halves in natural juice, drained

caster sugar to taste (optional)

1 Line a lightly oiled 500g (1lb) loaf tin with cling film. Melt chocolate with single cream over barely simmering water, stirring occasionally. Leave to cool.

2 Whip double cream to soft peaks. Whisk in chocolate mixture and liqueur. Fold in half the crushed ratafias. Spoon into the prepared tin; level the top. Cover with foil and freeze overnight until firm.

3 Meanwhile make sauce. Purée apricots in a blender or food processor. Add caster sugar if required. Spoon into a jug; chill.

4 About 30 minutes before serving, invert the frozen dessert onto a chilled serving plate. Remove the cling film. Using a palette knife, press remaining ratafia crumbs over top and sides. Refrigerate until ready to serve.

5 To decorate the slice, place strips of greaseproof paper diagonally across the top. Dust with icing sugar, then carefully remove strips to reveal the pattern. Serve at once, with the apricot sauce.

Serves 6

Chocolate Cherry Cheesecake

90g (3oz) plain chocolate

75g (2¹/₂oz) butter

280g (9oz) digestive biscuits, crumbed

Filling and Topping

1 x 470g (15oz) can stoned black cherries in syrup

375g (12oz) full fat soft cheese

90g (3oz) caster sugar

2 eggs, separated

1-1¹/₂ tblspn kirsch

15g (¹/₂oz) powdered gelatine

3 tblspn cold water

300ml (10fl oz) whipping cream

1 tblspn arrowroot

125g (4oz) dark chocolate, to decorate

1 Line and grease a 23cm (9in) loose-bottomed cake tin. In a saucepan, melt the chocolate and butter over low heat, then mix with the biscuit crumbs. Spread the mixture evenly over the base of the tin, pressing down well. Chill.

2 Drain cherries, reserving syrup. Cut them in half and spread one third over the crumb base.

3 In a large bowl, beat cheese with caster sugar. Beat in egg yolks and add 1 tablespoon of the kirsch.

4 Sprinkle gelatine over the water in a cup. When spongy, melt over hot water. Cool slightly.

5 Whip cream to soft peaks. In a clean dry bowl whisk egg whites until stiff. Beat gelatine gradually into cheese mixture, then fold in whipped cream. Finally fold in egg whites. Turn filling onto chilled base; spread evenly. Chill for several hours or overnight.

6 Make a glaze. In a cup, mix the arrowroot with a little of the reserved syrup from the cherries. Pour remaining syrup into a pan. Add kirsch to taste. Bring to the boil, then stir in arrowroot mixture. Stir until mixture thickens and clears. Remove from the heat and set aside to cool slightly, stirring occasionally.

7 Remove cheesecake from tin. Decorate by piling the cherries in the centre and spooning a little of the glaze over the top. Complete the decoration by using the dark chocolate to make curls (page 5), arranging them in a circle around the cherries.

Serves 8

Chocolate Cherry Cheesecake

Hot Puddings and Pancakes

Some like chocolate hot – not just as a soothing bedtime drink but in puddings, sauces and soufflés. When the weather turns chilly, toss a pancake or two, add a creamy filling and a dollop of chocolate sauce and enjoy the sweet taste of culinary success.

Sensational Steamed Pudding

60g (2oz) butter, plus extra for greasing

90g (3oz) plain chocolate

155ml (5fl oz) milk

60g (2oz) caster sugar

2 eggs, separated

155g (5oz) fresh white breadcrumbs

¼ tspn ground cinnamon

1 tspn vanilla essence

2 tblspn Grand Marnier or other orange liqueur

600ml (1pt) hot custard

1 Grease a 900ml (1½pt) pudding basin generously with butter. In a medium saucepan, melt 60g (2oz) butter with chocolate over very gentle heat. Pour in milk and stir until blended.

2 Off heat, stir in caster sugar, egg yolks and breadcrumbs. Flavour with cinnamon and vanilla essence, mixing well.

3 In a clean dry bowl, whisk egg whites until stiff. Gently fold into chocolate crumb mixture, working quickly and lightly. Spoon into the prepared basin, cover with a double thickness of foil turned down over the rim. Tie foil in place with string.

4 Place the bowl in a steamer or on an inverted plate in a large saucepan. Pour in boiling water to a depth of 7.5cm (3in). Steam the pudding for 1½ hours, adding more water as necessary.

5 To serve, remove the foil from the pudding basin, then run a knife carefully around the pudding to release it. Invert it onto a heated plate. Stir the liqueur into the hot custard and serve in a jug with the hot pudding.

Serves 6-8

White Chocolate Gratin

This delicious pudding has three distinct layers. A crisp coconut and chocolate topping, a light soufflé centre and a creamy white chocolate sauce.

200g (7oz) white chocolate

2 tblspn single cream or milk

45g (1½oz) butter

4 eggs, separated

60g (2oz) caster sugar

30g (1oz) flour

1 tspn vanilla essence

Topping

30g (1oz) white chocolate, grated

30g (1oz) shredded coconut

1 Preheat oven to 180°C (350°F/ Gas 4). Grease a gratin dish. Melt white chocolate in a heatproof bowl with cream or milk (see page 4). Melt butter in a small saucepan. Using a hand-held electric mixer, beat melted butter into chocolate.

2 Whisk egg yolks with sugar until pale and creamy. Add chocolate mixture, flour and vanilla essence. Beat until smooth.

3 In a clean dry bowl whisk egg whites until peaks form. Beat a little of the egg white into the chocolate mixture to lighten it, then fold in the rest with a metal spoon.

4 Spoon the mixture into the prepared gratin dish, sprinkle with the grated white chocolate and shredded coconut and bake for 30 minutes. Serve at once.

Serves 6

Variation
Dark chocolate can be used instead of milk chocolate, if preferred and a mixture of grated chocolate and finely chopped hazelnuts used for the topping.

Sensational Steamed Pudding

Rum Chocolate Soufflé

3 eggs, separated, plus 1 egg white

6 tblspn icing sugar

2 tblspn plain flour

300ml (10fl oz) milk

60g (2oz) plain chocolate, grated

2 tblspn dark rum

pinch salt

Rum Sauce

2 tblspn cornflour

375ml (12fl oz) milk

1 tspn vanilla essence

2 egg yolks

60g (2oz) caster sugar

2 tblspn dark rum

1 Make the sauce. In a saucepan, mix cornflour to a cream with a little of the milk, then stir in remaining milk and vanilla. Bring to the boil, whisking constantly. Whisk egg yolks and sugar in a bowl until pale and fluffy; pour on boiling milk mixture, whisking constantly. Cover closely. When cool, chill sauce.

2 Preheat oven to 220°C (425°F/ Gas 7). Grease a 1.2 litre (2pt) soufflé dish. Put egg yolks, icing sugar and flour in a heavy-based saucepan. Off the heat, whisk until smooth. In a second pan, bring milk to the boil. Add milk to flour mixture in a steady stream, whisking constantly, then cook, stirring constantly until the custard is smooth and thick.

3 Off the heat, stir in grated chocolate and rum. Pour mixture into a large bowl. In a separate, dry bowl, whisk all the egg whites with the salt until stiff. Fold into hot custard, working swiftly.

4 Spoon mixture into the prepared dish. With a clean thumb, make a gutter on top of the mixture, between it and the dish. Bake for 25-30 minutes until well risen. Serve immediately, with the chilled rum sauce.

Serves 4

Chocolate Date Puddings

110g (3 1/2 oz) white chocolate

2 tblspn milk

2 eggs, separated

2 tblspn caster sugar

1 tblspn brandy (optional)

60g (2oz) walnuts, finely chopped

90g (3oz) pitted dates, chopped

8 digestive biscuits, crumbed

2 tblspn self-raising flour

30g (1oz) butter, melted

Chocolate Sauce

110g (3 1/2 oz) dark chocolate, grated

125ml (4fl oz) double cream

1 Preheat oven to 150°C (300°F/ Gas 2). Line and grease four 250ml (8fl oz) soufflé dishes.

2 Melt white chocolate with milk over hot water (page 4). In a mixing bowl, beat egg yolks with sugar and brandy until thick and pale. Stir in walnuts, dates, biscuit crumbs, melted chocolate, flour and melted butter. Mix well.

3 In a clean dry bowl, whisk egg whites until soft peaks form; fold into nut mixture. Divide between the prepared dishes. Bake for 45-60 minutes or until puddings are cooked through.

4 Meanwhile make the sauce. Combine chocolate and cream in a small heavy-based saucepan. Heat gently until chocolate melts, then beat until smooth.

5 To serve, invert each pudding on a dessert plate. Pour a puddle of sauce around each pudding and serve the remainder separately.

Serves 4

Kitchen Tip

Heat a baking sheet in the oven and place the soufflé dishes on this to promote even cooking.

Rum Chocolate Soufflé

Cinnamon Chocolate Pudding

Cinnamon Chocolate Pudding

60g (2oz) butter or margarine, plus extra for greasing

185g (6oz) self-raising flour

2 tspn ground cinnamon

60g (2oz) soft brown sugar

1 tblspn golden syrup

1 egg, beaten

155ml (5fl oz) milk

Sauce

1 tblspn cornflour

125g (4oz) soft brown sugar

30g (1oz) cocoa powder

300ml (10fl oz) milk

1 Preheat oven to 180°C (350°F/ Gas 4). Grease a 1.2 litre (2pt) baking dish. Sift flour and cinnamon together; set aside.

2 In a bowl, cream butter or margarine with sugar until light and fluffy. Beat in syrup and egg. Fold in flour mixture alternately with milk. Do not overmix as this will make the pudding heavy.

3 Spoon mixture into the prepared dish. Bake for 40-45 minutes or until a skewer inserted in the pudding comes out clean.

4 To make the sauce, mix cornflour, sugar and cocoa powder in a small pan. Stir in enough milk to make a paste, then add the remaining milk. Bring to the boil, whisking constantly, then lower the heat and simmer for 1-2 minutes. To serve, pour about one third of the sauce over the hot pudding. Offer the rest in a jug.

Serves 4-6

Self-saucing Chocolate Pudding

90g (3oz) self-raising flour

2 tblspn cocoa powder

pinch salt

250g (8oz) butter or margarine, softened

125g (4oz) caster sugar

1/2 tspn vanilla essence

2 eggs, lightly beaten

60ml (2fl oz) milk

Sauce

90g (3oz) soft brown sugar

2 tblspn cocoa powder

300ml (10fl oz) boiling water

1 Preheat oven to 180°C (350°F/ Gas 4). Lightly grease a baking dish. Sift flour, cocoa and salt together; set aside.

2 In a bowl, cream butter and sugar until light and fluffy, then beat in vanilla. Add eggs, a little at a time, beating after each addition.

3 Gradually stir in flour mixture and add enough milk to give a smooth dropping consistency. Spoon mixture into the prepared dish; level surface.

4 To make sauce, mix sugar and cocoa in a jug. Gradually add water, whisking until smooth. Pour sauce over surface of pudding. It will sink during baking so that the finished pudding will have a sponge topping over a delectable sauce. Bake for 40 minutes or until the sponge topping is well risen and firm. Serve hot.

Serves 4

Chocolate Crêpes with Coconut Filling

75g (2¹/₂oz) butter, melted

2 tblspn caster sugar

3 tblspn cocoa powder

1 tblspn instant coffee powder

4 tblspn boiling water

3 eggs

250ml (8fl oz) milk

125g (4oz) plain flour

Coconut Filling

1 egg yolk

60ml (2fl oz) milk

155ml (5fl oz) coconut cream

5 tspn cornflour

75g (2¹/₂oz) caster sugar

1 Start by making the filling. Whisk egg yolk and milk in a small bowl. Combine coconut cream, cornflour and sugar in a saucepan. Bring to the boil, whisking constantly, then lower the heat to a bare simmer. Add egg yolk and milk; stir until mixture thickens. Cover and allow to cool.

2 Meanwhile combine butter, sugar and cocoa in a food processor. Process until smooth. Dissolve coffee powder in boiling water; add to cocoa mixture with eggs. Process briefly, then add milk and flour and process until smooth. Allow batter to rest at room temperature for 1 hour.

3 Heat a greased crêpe pan over moderate heat. Pour in about 2 tablespoons of batter, tilting pan to cover bottom thinly. Cook over moderate heat until browned underneath, then turn and cook the other side briefly. Repeat with remaining batter to make a total of 12 crêpes, keeping cooked crêpes warm in a low oven.

4 Place a generous tablespoon of the coconut filling on each crêpe and roll up. Place 2 crêpes on each of 6 dessert plates. Serve the filled crêpes at once.

Serves 6

Sweet Cheese Crêpes with Chocolate Sauce

90g (3oz) plain flour

¹/₂ tspn salt

2 eggs, beaten

2 tblspn melted butter or oil

155ml (5fl oz) milk

oil for frying

Chocolate Sauce (see Chocolate Date Puddings, page 22)

Filling

75g (2¹/₂oz) caster sugar

3 egg yolks

375g (12oz) full fat soft cheese

185g (6oz) ricotta cheese

185g (6oz) cream cheese

¹/₄ tspn vanilla essence

1 Sift flour and salt into a bowl. Make a well in the centre and add eggs, butter or oil and milk. Gradually mix to make a smooth batter.

2 Heat a greased crêpe pan over moderate heat. Pour in about 2 tablespoons of batter, tilting pan to cover bottom thinly. Cook over moderate heat until browned underneath, then turn and cook the other side briefly. Repeat with remaining batter to make 12 crêpes.

3 Make the filling. In a bowl, combine caster sugar, egg yolks, cheeses and vanilla essence. Beat until smooth. Chill for 30 minutes.

4 Preheat oven to 180°C (350°F/ Gas 4). Make the chocolate sauce and keep it hot over simmering water.

5 Divide chilled cheese mixture between crêpes. Roll them up and arrange in a single layer in a shallow baking dish. Bake for 10 minutes until warmed through. Serve 2 crêpes per person. Pour a little of the hot chocolate sauce over each portion and serve the rest separately.

Serves 6

Chocolate Dip

Illustrated on cover
This is very much a last-minute dessert, best prepared just before being served.

440g (14oz) dark chocolate, broken into squares

300ml (10fl oz) double cream

4 tblspn chocolate or coffee liqueur

60g (2oz) unsalted butter, cubed

For Dipping

selection of fresh fruit, eg bananas, strawberries, grapes, apples, clementines

2 tblspn lemon juice

16 pink marshmallows

16 x 5cm (2in) cubes of plain sponge cake

1 x 375g (12oz) can mandarin orange segments, drained

16 maraschino cherries

1 Prepare fruit for dipping. Peel bananas and slice into a bowl. Hull strawberries and grapes. Core but do not peel apples; slice them into the bowl and toss, with the bananas, in lemon juice to prevent discoloration.

2 To make dip, combine chocolate, cream and liqueur in a heat proof bowl. Bring a saucepan of water to the boil, lower the heat to a bare simmer, and place the bowl on top of the pan. Heat, stirring occasionally, until the chocolate has melted and the mixture is hot. Do not allow it to boil. Add the butter cubes and stir until melted. Leaving the bowl in place, remove the pan from the heat.

3 Drain banana and apple slices and arrange them, with the marshmallows, cake and remaining fruit, on 8 individual dessert plates. Divide the chocolate sauce between 8 ramekins and place one in the centre of each plate. Serve at once, with fondue forks for spearing the dippers.

Serves 8

Sweet Cheese Crêpes with Chocolate Sauce

DREAMY CHOCOLATE CAKES

Guests are guaranteed to ask for second slices of these mouthwatering cakes.
Black Forest Gâteau, Chocolate Fudge Cake, Gâteau Esterel or
Chocolate Chip Ring – who could resist these tempting treats?

Snowflake Cake

375g (12oz) butter

375g (12oz) caster sugar

6 eggs

375g (12oz) self-raising flour

140g (4¹/₂oz) ground almonds

White Fudge Icing

90g (3oz) butter

125g (4oz) white chocolate

4 tblspn milk

375g (12oz) icing sugar

Filling and Decoration

315g (10oz) hazelnut chocolate spread

125g (4oz) white chocolate caraque (page 5)

1 Preheat oven to 180°C (350°F/ Gas 4). Line and grease three 20cm (8in) sandwich cake tins.

2 Using one third of the cake ingredients each time, make three layers as follows: Cream butter with sugar in a mixing bowl. Beat in eggs with a little flour to prevent curdling, then add remaining flour and ground nuts. Spoon into prepared tin and level the surface.

3 Bake the cake layers for 30-35 minutes or until cooked through. Cool on a wire rack.

4 Sandwich layers together, using chocolate hazelnut spread. To make the icing, melt butter and white chocolate with milk, stirring until smooth. Stir in icing sugar, then beat until smooth and glossy. Cool slightly, then use to cover top and sides of cake. Decorate with white chocolate caraque.

Serves 8

Caraque Cake

185g (6oz) soft margarine

185g (6oz) caster sugar

3 eggs

170g (5¹/₂oz) self-raising flour

15g (¹/₂oz) cocoa powder

1 tspn baking powder

Filling

250ml (8fl oz) double cream

1 tspn icing sugar

few drops vanilla essence

Glaze and Topping

4 tblspn smooth apricot jam

1 tblspn lemon juice

250g (8oz) dark chocolate caraque (page 5)

sifted icing sugar

1 Preheat oven to 160°C (325°F/ Gas 3). Base line and grease two 20cm (8in) sandwich cake tins. Using a hand-held electric mixer, beat all the cake ingredients together in a mixing bowl for 2-3 minutes or until light and fluffy. Divide between prepared tins and bake for 25-30 minutes or until cooked through. Cool on a wire rack.

2 Whip cream with icing sugar and vanilla. Use to sandwich cake layers together.

3 In a small saucepan, melt the apricot jam in the lemon juice, stirring until smooth. Brush over the top and sides of the cake.

4 Reserving the best caraque curls for the top, carefully pat caraque all over the glazed cake to cover it thickly. Dust with icing sugar and serve as soon as possible.

Serves 6-8

Left: Snowflake Cake
Right: Caraque Cake

Devil's Food Cake

90g (3oz) dark chocolate

280g (9oz) plain flour

2 tspn bicarbonate of soda

1/2 tspn salt

125g (4oz) butter, softened

500g (1lb) soft brown sugar

3 eggs

1 tspn vanilla essence

125ml (4 fl oz) buttermilk or soured milk (see Kitchen Tip)

250ml (8fl oz) boiling water

Rich Chocolate Frosting

125g (4oz) dark chocolate

350g (12oz) icing sugar

2 egg whites

1/4 tspn cream of tartar

1 Preheat oven to 180°C (350°F/ Gas 4). Base line and grease three 20cm (8in) sandwich cake tins. Melt chocolate over hot water (see page 4). Sift flour with bicarbonate of soda and salt; set the bowl aside.

2 Combine butter, sugar, eggs and vanilla essence in a mixing bowl. Using a hand-held electric mixer, beat for about 5 minutes or until the mixture is pale and fluffy. Gradually beat in melted chocolate.

3 Beat in flour mixture alternately with buttermilk or soured milk. Do not overbeat or the cake will be heavy. Finally, beat in boiling water to make a fairly thin cake mixture.

4 Divide the mixture between the prepared tins. Bake for 30-35 minutes or until the cakes shrink slightly from the sides of the tins and the surface of each springs back when lightly pressed.

5 Cool in tins for 5 minutes, then turn out on wire racks to cool completely.

6 Make the frosting. Melt chocolate over hot water (page 4). Combine icing sugar, egg whites and cream or tartar in a large heatproof bowl. Place over a large pan of gently simmering water.

7 Using a hand-held electric mixer, beat mixture until it forms soft peaks. This will take about 8-10 minutes. Remove bowl from heat. Gradually whisk in melted chocolate.

8 Use some of the frosting to sandwich the cake layers together and spread the rest over the top and sides of the cake, swirling it with a palette knife.

Serves 8

Kitchen Tip
If buttermilk is not available, sour 125ml (4fl oz) milk by adding 1 teaspoon lemon juice.

No-egg Chocolate Cake

A simply delicious cake for anyone who is unable to tolerate eggs.

155g (5oz) self-raising flour

30g (1oz) cocoa powder

1 1/2 tspn baking powder

3/4 tspn bicarbonate of soda

60g (2oz) butter

2 tblspn molasses

2 tblspn soft brown sugar

185ml (6fl oz) milk

1 Preheat oven to 180°C (350°F/ Gas 4). Base line and grease a 20cm (8in) round cake tin.

2 Sift flour, cocoa, baking powder and bicarbonate of soda together in a mixing bowl.

3 Melt butter and molasses with sugar over very low heat, stirring. Off heat, stir in milk.

4 Make a well in the centre of the dry ingredients and add the liquid. Beat to a smooth batter. Pour into tin and bake for 30 minutes or until a skewer inserted in the centre comes out clean.

5 Cool cake in tin for 5 minutes, then invert on a wire rack. Top with plain or chocolate icing of own choice.

Serves 6-8

Mocha Layer Cake

220g (7oz) self-raising flour

30g (1oz) cocoa powder

2 tspn instant coffee powder

220g (7oz) butter

220g (7oz) caster sugar

4 eggs, beaten

walnut halves to decorate

Buttercream

2 tblspn cocoa powder

2 tblspn boiling water

1 tspn coffee essence

125g (4oz) butter, softened

125g (4oz) icing sugar, sifted

1 Preheat oven to 190°C (375°F/ Gas 5). Base line and grease two 18cm (7in) sandwich cake tins. Sift flour, cocoa powder and instant coffee powder together.

2 Cream butter and sugar in a mixing bowl until light and fluffy. Add eggs one at a time, beating after each addition and adding a little of the flour mixture if the mixture shows signs of curdling. Fold in remaining flour mixture lightly but thoroughly; do not beat or cake will be heavy.

3 Divide cake mixture between prepared tins, levelling the tops, then making a shallow hollow in the centre of each. Bake for 30 minutes or until a skewer inserted in the centre comes out clean. Cool the cakes in the tins for 5 minutes, then turn out on wire racks to cool completely.

4 Make buttercream. Dissolve cocoa powder in boiling water, then stir in coffee essence. Beat butter with icing sugar in a bowl, then gradually beat in enough of the cocoa mixture to make a creamy icing.

5 Sandwich the layers together with a little of the buttercream and use the rest to cover the top of the cake. Decorate with the walnut halves.

Serves 8

Mocha Layer Cake

Black Forest Gâteau

Mass production – not always successful – has dented the reputation of this magnificent cake. This version, which combines feather-light sponge with cherries, a kirsch-flavoured syrup and cream, is one of the finest.

155g (5oz) plain flour

2 tspn bicarbonate of soda

1 tspn instant coffee powder

1 tblspn cocoa powder

6 eggs, separated

155g (5oz) caster sugar

1 tspn lemon juice

90g (3oz) plain chocolate, finely grated

melted butter for greasing

Filling

125g (4oz) granulated sugar

600ml (1pt) water

1 kg (2lb) Morello cherries, stoned

155ml (5fl oz) kirsch

450ml (¾pt) double cream

3 tblspn icing sugar

25g (1oz) chocolate, coarsely grated or flaked, for decoration

1 Start making cherry filling. Combine granulated sugar and measured water in a heavy-based saucepan. Heat gently until sugar has dissolved, then bring to the boil and boil rapidly for 2 minutes without stirring. Lower the heat, add cherries and poach for 10 minutes.

2 Remove cherries with a slotted spoon; cool. Boil syrup rapidly for 10 minutes to reduce and thicken. Remove from the heat, measure out 90ml (3fl oz) and leave to cool.

3 Preheat oven to 180°C (350°F/ Gas 4). Base line and grease two 23cm (9in) sandwich cake tins. Sift dry ingredients together and set aside.

4 Combine egg yolks and sugar in a heatproof bowl. Set over simmering water and whisk until mixture is thick enough to hold the trail of the whisk for 3 seconds after the beaters are lifted. Whisk in lemon juice and chocolate. Remove the bowl from the heat.

5 Whisk egg whites in a clean dry bowl until soft peaks form. Stir 2 tablespoons of the whisked egg white into the chocolate mixture to lighten it, then fold in a quarter of the remaining egg white.

6 Sift over 2 tablespoons of the flour mixture and carefully fold in. Repeat process until all the ingredients have been added.

7 Divide mixture between cake tins. Bake for 25 minutes or until tops spring back when gently pressed. Cool in tins for 10 minutes, then invert cakes on a wire rack to cool completely.

8 Pat cherries dry with paper towels; set 8 aside for decoration. Add 125ml (4fl oz) of the kirsch to the reserved cherry syrup.

9 Whip double cream with icing sugar and remaining kirsch to soft peaks. Split each sponge in 2 horizontally. Place one of the bottom layers on a plate. Sprinkle with one third of the kirsch-flavoured syrup, cover with about a quarter of the cream; add about half the cherries, pressing them into the cream. Add a second sponge layer, sprinkle with more syrup, add a layer of cream and the rest of the cherries. Place the third layer on top, sprinkle with the rest of the syrup and spread with whipped cream. Finally add the top layer.

10 Spoon a small amount of the remaining cream into a piping bag fitted with a star nozzle; spread the rest over the top and sides of the cake. Pipe 16 cream rosettes around the rim of the cake.

Black Forest Gâteau

Marble Cake

Fill the centre with grated chocolate and stud alternate cream rosettes with the reserved cherries. Chill for 1 hour before serving.

Serves 8-10

Kitchen Tip

To save time, canned black cherries can be used. You will need two 440g (14oz) cans. Use 90ml (3fl oz) of the syrup in place of the home-made syrup in the recipe.

Marble Cake

185g (6oz) softened butter or margarine, plus extra for greasing

2 tblspn ground almonds

185g (6oz) caster sugar

3 eggs, lightly beaten

90g (3oz) plain flour

90g (3oz) self-raising flour

1 tblspn cocoa powder

1 tspn vanilla essence

1 Preheat oven to 180°C (350°F/ Gas 4). Grease a 1kg (2lb) loaf tin generously with butter, then add the almonds. Tip and tilt the tin to coat the sides and base evenly, then tap out any excess.

2 Cream butter and sugar in a mixing bowl until pale and fluffy. Add eggs, a little at a time, beating after each addition and adding a little flour if the mixture shows signs of curdling.

3 Sift flours into the mixture; fold in with a large metal spoon. Put half the mixture into a second bowl, sift in the cocoa powder and fold it in. Add vanilla to the remaining cake mixture.

4 Spread half the vanilla mixture in the prepared tin. Level the surface. Cover with half the cocoa mixture. Repeat the layers. There is no need to draw a skewer through the mixture as the marbling will occur naturally as the cake rises.

4 Bake for 45-55 minutes or until a skewer inserted into the cake comes out clean. If the cake starts to overbrown, cover with foil or greaseproof paper after 30 minutes baking.

5 Let the cake cool in the tin for 5 minutes, then invert it on a wire rack to cool completely.

Serves 8-10

Variation

Marble cakes are great fun to make. If preferred, divide the mixture between three bowls, flavouring one with the cocoa mixture, another with the vanilla and tinting the third a pale pink with food colouring. When layering the mixtures in the tin, use chocolate, vanilla, then pink, followed by vanilla, pink and chocolate. Alternatively, add alternate spoonfuls of mixture to the tin, then draw a skewer through several times to mix them.

Chocolate Victoria Sponge

250g (8oz) butter, softened

250g (8oz) caster sugar

1/2 tspn vanilla essence

1/2 tspn grated lemon rind

4 eggs

220g (7oz) plain flour

30g (1oz) cocoa powder

2 tspn baking powder

jam and whipped cream for filling

icing sugar to decorate

1 Preheat oven to 180°C (350°F/ Gas 4). Base line and grease two 19cm (7 1/2in) sandwich cake tins.

2 In a large mixing bowl, cream butter with caster sugar. Add vanilla essence and grated lemon rind. Beat until pale and fluffy.

3 In a separate bowl, whisk eggs until pale and frothy. Add eggs to creamed mixture, a little at a time, beating well after each addition, and adding a little flour if the mixture shows signs of curdling.

4 Sift flour, cocoa and baking powder over creamed mixture a little at a time, folding each addition in lightly but thoroughly with a large metal spoon.

5 Divide mixture between the prepared cake tins and level the surfaces. Bake for 25 minutes or until the cakes have shrunk away slightly from the sides of the the tins. When lightly pressed with a finger, the tops should spring back into shape.

6 Cool cake layers in tins for 2 minutes, then invert onto a clean tea towel. Peel off paper linings and invert cakes onto a wire rack, right side up, to cool.

7 When layers are cold, sandwich with slightly warmed jam and whipped cream. Place a paper doily on top of cake and dust lightly with icing sugar. Carefully remove doily to reveal pattern.

Serves 6-8

Variation
If preferred, the cake can be filled with hazelnut chocolate spread and cream.

Chocolate Victoria Sponge

Gâteau Esterel

Gâteau Esterel

1 tblspn dried yeast

4 tblspn lukewarm water

185g (6oz) butter

4 eggs

250g (8oz) caster sugar

250g (8oz) plain flour

8 tblspn orange marmalade

250g (8oz) plain chocolate, in squares

1 tblspn Cointreau or other orange liqueur

Syrup

125g (4oz) sugar

250ml (8fl oz) water

3 tblspn Cointreau or other orange liqueur

1 Preheat oven to 200°C (400°F/ Gas 6). Lightly grease a 20cm (8in) savarin mould or ring cake tin. Sprinkle yeast over lukewarm water in a small bowl. Set aside for about 5 minutes until frothy, then stir until dissolved. Melt butter.

2 In a mixing bowl, whisk eggs and sugar until light and fluffy. Sift over flour and fold in lightly but thoroughly, then fold in melted butter and yeast mixture. Pour into mould or tin; bake for 10 minutes.

3 Lower oven temperature to 180°C (350°F/Gas 4). Cook cake for 25 minutes more. Cool.

4 Combine sugar and measured water in a small pan. Heat, stirring, until sugar dissolves, then boil until syrup registers 110°C (225°F) on a sugar thermometer. Stir in Cointreau. Cool.

5 Cut cake in half horizontally. Set aside 3 tablespoons of the syrup and use the rest to moisten the cut sides of both cake halves. Sandwich cake halves together with marmalade. Place on a platter.

6 Melt chocolate over hot water (see page 4). Stir in reserved syrup and Cointreau, then beat until smooth. Pour over cake, spreading swiftly to cover.

Serves 6

Chocolate Swiss Roll

3 eggs

90g (3oz) caster sugar, plus extra for sprinkling

1 tspn vanilla essence

60g (2oz) plain flour

pinch salt

25g (1oz) cocoa powder

icing sugar to decorate

Filling

125g (4oz) drained canned morello cherries

3 tblspn kirsch

155g (5oz) plain chocolate, broken into squares

155ml (5fl oz) double cream

1 Prepare cherries for filling by marinating them in the kirsch in a small bowl for 3-4 hours.

2 Preheat oven to 200°C (400°F/ Gas 6). Line and grease a 33 x 23cm (13 x 9in) Swiss roll tin.

3 Combine the eggs, sugar and vanilla essence in a large heat-proof bowl. Place over simmering water and whisk for 10 minutes until mixture is very thick and pale. Off heat, continue to whisk for 5 minutes or until mixture is cold.

4 Sift flour, salt and cocoa onto a plate. Sift again on top of egg mixture. Fold in with a large metal spoon. Pour into the prepared tin and level the surface.

5 Bake for 12-15 minutes or until the sponge sprinks slightly from the sides of the tin, and the top springs back when lightly pressed.

6 Have ready a piece of grease-proof paper slightly larger than the sponge. Lay it flat on the work surface and sprinkle it lightly with caster sugar. Turn the sponge onto the paper, peel off the lining paper and trim the edges.

7 Lay a second piece of grease-proof paper on top of the sponge. While still warm, roll up the sponge from one short edge, keeping the paper inside. Cool.

8 Melt chocolate (page 4) and allow to cool slightly. Whip cream until stiff, then fold in chocolate.

9 Carefully unroll sponge, discarding paper, and spread with a little of the chocolate cream. Drain marinated cherries and spread them over cream. Roll sponge up again, place on a plate and spread with remaining chocolate cream. Dust lightly with icing sugar.

Serves 6

Cherry and Chocolate Chip Ring

125g (4oz) butter, softened

125g (4oz) golden granulated sugar

2 eggs, beaten

250g (8oz) self-raising flour

90g (3oz) glacé cherries, chopped

60g (2oz) chocolate chips

60-90ml (2-3fl oz) natural low fat yogurt or milk

1 Preheat oven to 180°C (350°F/ Gas 4). Grease a 900ml (1 1/2pt) ring mould or tin.

2 In a mixing bowl cream butter and sugar until light and fluffy. Gradually add eggs, beating after each addition. Add a little flour if mixture shows signs of curdling.

3 Combine flour, chopped cherries and chocolate chips. Add to mixing bowl and fold into creamed mixture with a metal spoon. Add enough yogurt or milk to give a soft dropping consistency.

4 Scrape into prepared mould or tin. Bake for 50-60 minutes or until a skewer inserted in the cake comes out clean. Cool in the tin for 10 minutes, then invert on a wire rack to cool completely.

Serves 8-10

Kitchen Tip
Freeze slices of this cake, individually wrapped, for lunch boxes. Simply pop a frozen slice in a box in the morning and it will have thawed by break or lunch time.

Chocolate Swiss Roll

Chocolate Fudge Cake

Chocolate Fudge Cake

375g (12oz) plain flour

1 tbsp baking powder

250g (8oz) butter, softened, or soft margarine

375g (12oz) soft brown sugar

4 eggs, lightly beaten

4 tblspn golden syrup

125g (4oz) cocoa powder

185ml (6fl oz) warm water

155ml (5fl oz) natural low fat yogurt

Fudge Icing

250g (8oz) plain chocolate, broken into squares

125g (4oz) butter, diced

2 eggs

250g (8oz) icing sugar

1 Preheat oven to 150°C (300°F/ Gas 2). Line and grease a deep 20cm (8in) round cake tin. Sift flour and baking powder together.

2 In a mixing bowl, beat the butter or margarine and sugar until pale and fluffy. Add eggs gradually, beating after each addition and adding a little flour if mixture shows signs of curdling.

3 Stir in syrup. In a small bowl, mix cocoa to a paste with measured water. Beat into creamed mixture.

4 Using a large metal tablespoon, fold in half the sifted flour mixture, using a figure-of-eight action. Fold in yogurt, then fold in remaining flour mixture until just combined. Scrape mixture into prepared tin. Level the surface.

5 Bake for 1¼-1½ hours. Cool briefly in tin, then invert on a wire rack to cool completely.

6 Make icing. In a large heatproof bowl over simmering water, melt chocolate and butter. Stir, leave to cool for 5 minutes, then beat in eggs, one at a time, until smooth. Add icing sugar, beating until smooth. Continue beating until mixture is thick and spreadable, see Kitchen Tip.

8 Use a little of the icing to sandwich the cake layers together, then spread the rest over the top and sides of the cake.

Serves 8-10

Kitchen Tip
If icing is too thin to spread, place it in the refrigerator. It will thicken on chilling. Beat it lightly before using it to ice the cake.

SMALL CAKES AND BISCUITS

Success on a plate is positively guaranteed with these delicious small cakes and biscuits. Whether your family plumps for cup cakes, chewy brownies or crisp chocolate chip cookies, be sure to keep the cake tin and biscuit barrel brimming.

Quick Chocolate Cup Cakes

125g (4oz) self-raising flour

30g (1oz) cocoa powder

125g (4oz) soft margarine

125 g (4oz) caster sugar

2 eggs

1/4 tspn vanilla essence

Icing and Decoration

250g (8oz) icing sugar

2-3 tblspn warm water

few drops vanilla essence

chocolate vermicelli, hundreds and thousands, quartered glacé cherries, silver dragees or other decorations to finish

1 Preheat oven to 180°C (350°F/ Gas 4). Support 20 paper cup cake cases in 2 tartlet or muffin trays.

2 Sift flour and cocoa into a mixing bowl. Add margarine, caster sugar, eggs and vanilla essence. Beat with a wooden spoon for 1-2 minutes until evenly combined.

3 Divide mixture equally between paper cases. Bake for 15 minutes or until risen and springy to the touch, then cool in the cases on a wire rack.

4 Make icing. Sift icing sugar into a bowl, then stir in just enough water to give a smooth coating consistency. Stir in vanilla essence.

5 Using a small palette knife, spread icing over cakes. Add chosen decorations while icing is still soft, then leave to set.

Makes 20

Brownies

125g (4oz) dark chocolate, broken into squares

90g (3oz) butter, diced

2 eggs

185g (6oz) dark brown sugar

125g (4oz) plain flour

60g (2oz) pecan nuts

1 tspn vanilla essence

1 Preheat oven to 180°C (350°F/ Gas 4). Base line and lightly grease an 18cm (7in) square cake tin.

2 Melt chocolate and butter in a large heatproof bowl over simmering water. Remove from the heat and cool slightly.

3 In a separate bowl, whisk eggs with sugar until pale and fluffy. Beat into chocolate mixture.

4 Sift flour over chocolate mixture; fold in lightly but thoroughly. Chop the nuts and stir them into the mixture with the vanilla essence.

5 Scrape the mixture into the prepared tin. Bake for 25-30 minutes.

6 Leave the brownies in the tin until cold, then invert onto a board, remove the lining paper and cut into squares or bars.

Makes 9 or 12

Chocolate Oaties

125g (4oz) butter, diced

125g (4oz) caster sugar

2 tblspn milk

few drops of vanilla essence

30g (1oz) cocoa powder

185g (6oz) porridge oats

hundreds and thousands or quartered glacé cherries to decorate

1 Combine butter, sugar, milk and vanilla essence in a heavy-based saucepan. Stir over low heat until butter has melted and sugar has dissolved completely, then bring to just below boiling point.

2 Off heat, stir in cocoa and oats. Mix well until evenly blended.

3 Arrange 20 small paper sweet cases on a tray. Divide the mixture between the cases. Decorate and refrigerate for 15 minutes before serving.

Makes 20

Chocolate Oaties

Ginger Chocolate Bars

125g (4oz) soft margarine

185g (6oz) soft brown sugar

3 eggs

1 tspn vanilla essence

250g (8oz) self-raising flour

1 tblspn ground ginger

185g (6oz) plain chocolate, grated

185g (6oz) currants

Glaze

155g (5oz) chocolate, broken into squares

30g (1oz) butter, diced

1 tblspn golden syrup

1 Preheat oven to 180°C (350°F/ Gas 4). Grease a 20cm (8in) square cake tin.

2 Combine margarine, sugar, eggs, vanilla essence, flour and ginger in a mixing bowl. Beat with a hand-held electric mixer until creamy. Stir in chocolate and currants, mixing well.

3 Spoon mixture into prepared tin; smooth the surface. Bake for 25-30 minutes or until a skewer inserted in the cake comes out clean and dry.

4 Cool cake in tin. Make glaze by melting chocolate with butter over hot water, then stirring in golden syrup. Spread glaze over cake; set aside.

5 When glaze has set, cut cake into squares.

Makes 16

Florins

90g (3oz) cocoa powder

220g (7oz) ground almonds

155g (5oz) caster sugar

pinch salt

30g (1oz) plain flour

2 eggs

90g (3oz) icing sugar

1 Line and grease 2 baking sheets. Mix cocoa, ground almonds, sugar, salt and flour in a bowl.

2 Stir in eggs with a wooden spoon, working mixture to a soft, sticky dough. Shape into a ball, cover and chill for 30 minutes.

3 Preheat oven to 180°C (350°F/ Gas 4). Sift icing sugar into a bowl. Dip fingers into icing sugar, pinch off walnut-sized pieces of dough. Place on prepared baking sheets, leaving room for spreading.

4 Bake biscuits for 12-15 minutes. Using a palette knife, transfer to a wire rack to cool. Sift remaining icing sugar over biscuits.

Makes about 48

Florentines

90g (3oz) butter, diced

60ml (2fl oz) golden syrup

2 tblspn plain flour

3 tblspn sultanas, halved

60g (2oz) glacé cherries, quartered

90g (3oz) flaked almonds

1 tspn lemon juice

125g (4oz) dark chocolate, broken into squares

1 Preheat oven to 180°C (350°F/ Gas 4). Base line 4 baking sheets neatly with nonstick baking parchment.

2 Melt butter with syrup in a heavy-bottomed saucepan, stirring as butter melts to make a smooth mixture. Cool slightly.

3 Stir flour into mixture with a metal spoon, then add sultanas, cherries, almonds and lemon juice. Stir until just combined.

4 Using a teaspoon, drop spoonfuls of the mixture onto the prepared baking sheets, leaving about 10cm (4in) between each spoonful to allow for spreading. Bake for 15 minutes. Cool on baking sheets, then carefully remove from paper.

5 Melt chocolate over hot water (see page 4). Cool slightly, then spread the underside of each biscuit with melted chocolate and arrange, chocolate side up, on wire racks. When the chocolate on each biscuit is on the point of setting, mark it in wavy lines with the tines of a fork. Leave the florentines on the racks in a cool place (not the refrigerator) until the chocolate has set completely.

Makes about 20

Whirls

185g (6oz) self-raising flour

30g (1oz) cocoa powder

185g (6oz) soft margarine

60g (2oz) icing sugar

1/4 tspn vanilla essence

20-24 roasted hazelnuts

1 Preheat oven to 160°C (325°F/ Gas 3). Grease 3 large baking sheets. Sift flour and cocoa into a mixing bowl.

2 Cream margarine and icing sugar in a mixing bowl until light and fluffy. Beat in flour mixture, a little at a time, then beat in vanilla essence.

3 Spoon mixture into a piping bag fitted with a large star nozzle. Pipe about 7 swirls, each about 5cm (2in) across, on each baking sheet, leaving a little room for spreading.

4 Place a hazelnut in the centre of each swirl. Bake for 15-20 minutes until biscuits are just firm.

5 Cool the biscuits for 2 minutes on baking sheets, then transfer carefully to wire racks until cold.

Makes 20-22

Kitchen Tip
Top the biscuits with glacé cherries or almonds if preferred. Whirls make perfect presents. Pack them carefully in a tin or box, separating the layers with paper towels.

Whirls

Chocolate Chip Cookies

125g (4oz) butter

110g (3¹/₂oz) granulated sugar

110g (3¹/₂oz) soft brown sugar

1 egg

¹/₂ tspn vanilla essence

185g (6oz) plain flour

¹/₂ tspn salt

¹/₂ tspn baking powder

60g (2oz) walnuts or pecan nuts, finely chopped

125g (4oz) chocolate chips

1 Preheat oven to 190°C (375°F/ Gas 5). Grease 3-4 large baking sheets.

2 Cream butter with both sugars in a large mixing bowl until light and fluffy. Beat in egg and vanilla essence.

3 Sift flour, salt and baking powder over mixture. Stir in, then beat until smooth. Stir in nuts and chocolate chips making sure that they are well distributed.

4 Using a teaspoon, drop spoonfuls of the mixture onto the prepared baking sheets, leaving space for spreading.

5 Bake for 10-15 minutes or until biscuits are lightly browned. Cool for 2 minutes on baking sheets, then transfer carefully to wire racks to cool completely.

Makes about 30

Crunchies

250g (8oz) plain digestive biscuits

60g (2oz) blanched almonds

60g (2oz) butter

220g (7oz) plain chocolate, broken into squares

3 tblspn golden syrup

60g (2oz) candied peel, chopped

30g (1oz) glacé cherries, chopped

icing sugar for dusting

1 Grease a shallow 18cm (7in) square cake tin. Chop biscuits into quite small pieces. If using a food processor, take care not to reduce them to fine crumbs. Chop nuts or in a food processor with a metal blade or by hand.

2 Combine butter, chocolate and golden syrup in a heavy-based saucepan. Heat gently, stirring until all the ingredients are well combined.

3 Remove pan from heat and stir in biscuits, nuts, candied peel and cherries. Mix well.

4 Scrape mixture into prepared tin, levelling the surface, and chill for several hours until set.

5 Cut the mixture into bars and place on a wire rack. Dust lightly with icing sugar.

Makes 18

Variations

Any sweet biscuit which is not too crisp can be used to make the bars. Rich tea biscuits and oat biscuits are suitable, as are hazelnut or almond biscuits. For a children's party use chocolate chip biscuits and add a melted chocolate topping before chilling the mixture.

Chocolate Chip Cookies and Crunchies

Walnut and Chocolate Cookies

Dipped Almond Bars

60g (2oz) soft margarine

125g (4oz) ground almonds

125g (4oz) caster sugar

2 eggs

2 tblspn plain flour

5 tblspn smooth apricot jam

125g (4oz) flaked almonds

90g (3oz) dark chocolate, broken into squares

1 Preheat oven to 190°C (375°F/ Gas 5). Base line and grease a 30 x 20cm (12 x 8in) Swiss roll tin.

2 Using a hand-held electric mixer, cream margarine with ground almonds and sugar in a mixing bowl until well combined. Beat in eggs one at a time, adding 1 tablespoon of flour with each.

3 Spoon mixture into tin, levelling the surface. Bake for 7 minutes or until golden brown.

4 Remove the tin from the oven and spread the jam over the top of the baked mixture. Sprinkle evenly with the almonds, then return the tin to the oven for 5 minutes more, or until the almonds are golden brown. Spread a sheet of nonstick baking parchment on the work surface.

5 Cool the bake for 3 minutes, then cut into bars. Leave on a wire rack until cold.

6 Melt chocolate over hot water (page 4). Dip half of each bar in chocolate, shaking off the excess, then place carefully on the prepared baking parchment. Leave in a cool place until set.

Makes 24

Walnut and Chocolate Cookies

90g (3oz) butter, softened

90g (3oz) caster sugar

90g (3oz) soft brown sugar

1 tspn vanilla essence

1 egg, beaten

125g (4oz) self-raising flour

1/2 tspn bicarbonate of soda

90g (3oz) walnuts, roughly chopped

90g (3oz) chocolate chips

1 Preheat oven to 190°C (375°F/ Gas 5). Grease 2-3 baking sheets.

2 Cream butter and sugars in a mixing bowl until fluffy. Beat in vanilla essence and egg, adding a little flour if mixture shows signs of curdling.

3 Sift flour and bicarbonate of soda over creamed mixture. Add walnuts and chocolate chips; fold in with a metal spoon.

4 Using a scant tablespoon of mixture each time, drop the mixture onto the prepared baking sheets, leaving about 5cm (2in) between each spoonful to allow to spreading.

5 Bake for 10-12 minutes until pale gold and firm to the touch. Cool on the baking sheets for 3-4 minutes, then carefully transfer cookies to a wire rack to cool completely.

Makes about 30

SWEETS AND TREATS

There's only one problem with these tasty chocolate treats – one is never enough. Make a few of your favourites for solitary self-indulgence or pack a selection in a pretty box or tin as a special gift.

Chocolate Nibbles

60g (2oz) plain chocolate, broken into squares

4 drained canned pineapple rings

15-30g (1/2-1oz) pistachio nuts, finely chopped

thinly pared rind of 1 large orange, cut into matchstick strips

90g (3oz) chocolate and orange cake covering, broken into squares

15 stoned dried dates

1 Melt chocolate in a heatproof bowl over hot water (page 4). Meanwhile, cut each pineapple ring into 6 equal pieces; dry on paper towels. Spread out nuts on a plate.

2 Have ready a sheet of nonstick baking parchment. Holding each piece of pineapple in turn between your fingers, dip the rounded end in melted chocolate, then in nuts. Place carefully on the parchment and leave to set.

3 Bring a small pan of water to the boil. Add strips of orange rind, bring back to the boil, then lower the heat and simmer for 1 minute. Drain thoroughly, then dry on paper towels. Set aside.

4 Melt cake covering over hot water, as for chocolate. Remove from the heat and stir. Spear each date in turn on the end of a skewer and coat in the chocolate, then use a fork to ease the coated date onto the sheet of parchment. Decorate with a few strips of orange rind. Leave in a cool place to set.

5 To serve, carefully remove the pineapple and date nibbles from the paper and arrange in paper sweet cases. These are best served on the day that they are made.

Makes about 40

Rum and Raisin Truffles

125g (4oz) seedless raisins

6 tblspn rum

8 trifle sponges

280g (9oz) plain chocolate, broken into pieces

90g (3oz) unsalted butter, diced

125g (4oz) ground almonds

125g (4oz) chocolate vermicelli

1 Put raisins in a small bowl. Add half the rum, cover and set aside to soak for 30 minutes.

2 Crumb trifle sponges, either by processing them briefly in a food processor, or by rubbing them on the coarse side of a grater. Melt chocolate with remaining rum (see page 4).

3 Gradually stir butter into melted chocolate mixture, making sure that each addition is absorbed before adding the next. Add sponge crumbs, almonds and soaked raisins, with any remaining rum. Mix well, then leave to cool. Chill if necessary – the mixture must be firm enough to shape.

4 Divide mixture into 24 walnut-sized pieces; roll into balls. Spread out vermicelli on a baking sheet. Add balls, a few at a time, rolling them in the vermicelli until well coated.

5 Arrange the truffles in plain or decorative small paper cases. Refrigerate until ready to serve.

Makes 24

Cherry Dreams

12 stoned cherries

3 tblspn cherry brandy

155g (5oz) plain chocolate, broken into squares

1 Soak the cherries in the cherry brandy for 2 hours. Drain, reserving brandy, and dry on paper towels.

2 Melt chocolate with reserved cherry brandy over hot water (page 4). Using half the mixture, and following the instructions on page 5, make 12 miniature chocolate cases.

3 When the cases have set, place one of the cherries in each. Warm the remaining chocolate, if necessary, to melt it, then top up each chocolate case, covering the cherries completely. Chill until set.

Makes 12

Walnut Wonders, Ginger Twirls

Walnut Wonders

30g (1oz) butter

2 tspn golden syrup

2 tblspn cocoa powder

2 tblspn boiling water

125g (4oz) sugar

1 tblspn double cream

1/2 tspn vanilla essence

125g (4oz) walnut halves

Syrup

4 tblspn sugar

2 tblspn water

1 Base line a baking sheet with nonstick baking parchment. Have ready about 24 paper sweet cases on a second baking sheet.

2 Melt butter with syrup in a heavy-based saucepan.Dissolve cocoa in boiling water and add to pan with sugar. Continue to heat, stirring to dissolve sugar.

3 Bring to the boil over low heat, stirring constantly. Add cream and continue to boil for about 6 minutes until mixture registers 115°F (235°C) on a sugar thermometer, see Kitchen Tip.

1 Off heat, add vanilla essence and beat until mixture thickens slightly. Half fill a large shallow dish with cold water.

2 Using a teaspoon, drop spoonfuls of the mixture into the water. By the time you add the fifth spoonful, the first should be ready for rolling.

3 Drain the piece of fudge, roll it to a ball and sandwich between 2 walnut halves. Put on the prepared baking sheet to set and repeat with remaining fudge and walnut halves. Place the baking sheet in the refrigerator while you make the syrup for coating.

4 In a small saucepan, heat sugar and measured water gently, stirring until sugar has dissolved. Raise heat and continue to cook until syrup is pale gold in colour. Remove the pan from the heat.

5 Using a cocktail stick, spear each sweetmeat in turn through the fudge filling; dip quickly in the hot syrup, shaking off excess. Immediately place in the paper sweet cases and chill for 2 hours until set.

Makes about 24

Kitchen Tip
If you do not have a sugar thermometer, test mixture by dropping about 1/2 teaspoon into a cup of iced water. Pour off water after a couple of seconds. If you can mould mixture between your fingers to make a soft ball, the fudge is ready.

Ginger Twirls

250g (8oz) plain chocolate

3 tblspn very strong black coffee

60g (2oz) butter, softened

2 egg yolks

2 tspn ginger wine

18 small pieces of stem ginger in syrup, drained

1 Melt chocolate in a heatproof bowl over hot water (see page 4). Using half the chocolate, and following the instructions on page 5, make 18 miniature chocolate cases. Chill until set.

2 Warm remaining chocolate, if necessary, to melt it, then stir in coffee. Cool slightly.

3 Peel away paper from chilled chocolate cases, then return them to the refrigerator.

4 Beat softened butter into the melted chocolate mixture, then stir in egg yolks and wine. Chill mixture until firm enough to pipe.

5 Drain ginger and dry on paper towels. Place one piece of ginger in each chocolate case. Spoon chocolate mixture into a piping bag fitted with a star nozzle. Fill each chocolate case with swirls of piped chocolate, covering ginger completely. Set twirls in fresh paper cases. Chill before serving.

Makes about 18

Variation
Use maraschino cherries and cherry brandy instead of stem ginger and ginger wine, or make a selection of these chocolate treats.

Chocolate-coated Hazelnuts

Illustrated on page 3

220g (7oz) dark chocolate

250g (8oz) roasted hazelnuts

1 Melt chocolate over hot water (see page 4). Add about 2 tablespoons hazelnuts. Stir to coat in chocolate.

2 Using 2 teaspoons, scoop up chocolate-coated nuts in clusters of 3 or 4; carefully transfer to small paper sweet cases. Repeat with remaining nuts. Leave in a cool place until set.

Makes about 30

Fudge

60g (2oz) plain chocolate, broken into squares

500g (1lb) sugar

155ml (5fl oz) milk

60g (2oz) butter, diced

1 Grease a 20cm (8in) square cake tin. Combine chocolate, sugar and milk in a heavy-based saucepan. Heat gently, stirring to dissolve sugar and chocolate.

2 Bring to the boil over low heat, stirring constantly. Continue to boil until mixture registers 115°F (235°C) on a sugar thermometer, see Kitchen Tip, page 44.

3 Remove pan from heat and set aside for 5 minutes. Beat in butter until melted. The mixture should be thick and smooth. Pour into the prepared cake tin and allow to cool and harden slightly before marking into squares. When cold, separate squares and remove from tin.

Makes about 48 pieces

Cheat's Walnut and Chocolate Fudge

45g (1½oz) soft brown sugar

125g (4oz) butter

3 tblspn golden syrup

250g (8oz) Madeira cake or plain sponge cake, crumbled

60g (2oz) cocoa powder

155g (5oz) walnut pieces, roughly chopped

1 Line a 15cm (6in) square cake tin neatly with nonstick baking parchment.

2 Combine sugar, butter and syrup in a saucepan. Heat gently, stirring until butter has melted and sugar has dissolved. Off heat, stir in cake crumbs, cocoa and nuts.

3 Scrape mixture into prepared tin. Dip a palette knife in boiling water and smooth the surface, then set mixture aside to cool. When cold, refrigerate for 3-4 hours until fudge is firm.

4 To serve, cut into cubes and place in paper sweet cases.

Makes about 36

Variations
This is a good natured mixture which can be varied according to what you have in the pantry. Try ginger cake, substituting half the golden syrup with syrup from a jar of stem ginger.

Fudge

Malted Milkshakes

8 ice cubes, crushed

500ml (16fl oz) block vanilla ice cream, cut into cubes

3 tblspn cocoa powder, sifted

2 tspn caster sugar

300ml (10fl oz) milk

3 tblspn malt extract (see Kitchen Tip)

To Serve (optional)

4 scoops extra vanilla ice cream

4 chocolate flakes

1 Chill 4 glass tumblers in the refrigerator for 30 minutes. Put half the ice and half the ice cream in a blender or food processor. Add half the cocoa, sugar, milk and malt. Blend or process for 2 minutes until frothy, resting motor after 1 minute.

2 Divide between 2 of the chilled tumblers. Use the remaining ingredients to make 2 more drinks in the same way.

3 For a luxury touch, top each malted milkshake with an extra scoop of vanilla ice cream and add a chocolate flake.

Serves 4

Kitchen Tip
Malt extract is a dark brown sticky syrup derived from barley. It is sold in chemists and health food shops.

Hot Chocolate

Illustrated on page 3

185g (6oz) plain chocolate, broken into squares

1 litre (1³/₄pt) milk

whipped cream and grated chocolate to serve

1 In a heavy-based saucepan over gentle heat, melt chocolate with just enough milk to moisten. Watch the mixture carefully - it must not get to hot or it will scorch.

2 In a separate pan, bring the rest of the milk to the boil.

3 Off heat, whisk boiling milk into melted chocolate until evenly

Malted Milkshake

blended and frothy. Divide between 4 heatproof glasses or mugs, top with whipped cream and grated chocolate and serve at once.

Serves 4

Variations
Viennese Chocolate: Allow the chocolate milk to cool, then whisk in 4 egg yolks. Return the flavoured milk to the pan and heat through gently, stirring constantly. Do not allow the milk to boil. Serve in heatproof glasses with whipped cream and grated dark chocolate.
Mochachoc: Melt the chocolate in 375ml (12fl oz) strong black coffee. Pour into a measuring jug and add boiling milk to make up to 1 litre (1³/₄pt). Whisk well, pour into heatproof glasses or mugs and serve with whipped cream.
Marshmallow Topper: Make the hot chocolate as in the main recipe, but top with white marshmallows instead of cream. The marshmallows will melt to form a delicious topping that is popular with children.

Chocolate Rum Punch

185g (6oz) sugar

60g (2oz) cocoa powder

500ml (16fl oz) milk

250ml (8fl oz) dark rum

250ml (8fl oz) single cream

125ml (4fl oz) orange liqueur

ice cubes to serve

1 Mix sugar and cocoa powder in a heavy-based saucepan. Gradually stir in milk until mixture is smooth. Bring to simmering point and simmer, stirring, for 1 minute. Allow mixture to cool.

2 Stir in rum, cream and orange liqueur. Refrigerate until chilled. Serve over ice cubes in punch cups or small tumblers.

Serves 10

USEFUL INFORMATION

Length

Centimetres	Inches	Centimetres	Inches
0.5 (5mm)	¼	18	7
1	½	20	8
2	¾	23	9
2.5	1	25	10
4	1½	30	12
5	2	35	14
6	2½	40	16
7.5	3	45	18
10	4	50	20
15	6	NB: 1cm = 10mm	

Metric/Imperial Conversion Chart
Mass (Weight)
(Approximate conversions for cookery purposes)

Metric	Imperial	Metric	Imperial
15g	½oz	315g	10oz
30g	1oz	350g	11oz
60g	2oz	375g	12oz (¾lb)
90g	3oz	410g	13oz
125g	4oz (¼lb)	440g	14oz
155g	5oz	470g	15oz
185g	6oz	500g (0.5kg)	16oz (1lb)
220g	7oz	750g	24oz (1½lb)
250g	8oz (½lb)	1000g (1kg)	32oz (2lb)
280g	9oz	1500g (1.5kg)	3lb

Metric Spoon Sizes
Metric Spoon Sizes

¼ teaspoon	= 1.25ml
½ teaspoon	= 2.5ml
1 teaspoon	= 5ml
1 tablespoon	=15ml

Liquids

Metric	Imperial
30ml	1fl oz
60ml	2fl oz
90ml	3fl oz
125ml	4fl oz
155ml	5fl oz (¼pt)
185ml	6fl oz
250ml	8fl oz
500ml	16fl oz
600ml	20fl oz (1pt)
750ml	1¼pt
1 litre	1¾pt
1.2 litres	2pt
1.5 litres	2½pt
1.8 litres	3pt
2 litres	3½pt
2.5 litres	4pt

Index

Editorial Coordination: Merehurst Limited
Cookery Editor: Jenni Fleetwood
Production Editor: Sheridan Packer
Production Manager: Anna Maguire
Design: Clive Dorman
Cover Photography: David Gill
Cover Home Economist: Maxine Clark
Photography: Pages 2, 4 and 5, Merehurst Limited.
All other photographs supplied by Marshall
Cavendish Picture Library, London.

Published by J.B. Fairfax Press Pty Limited
80-82 McLachlan Avenue
Rushcutters Bay, NSW 2011

Printed by Toppan Printing Co, Hong Kong
PRINTED IN HONG KONG

ISBN 1 86343 116 0 (set)
ISBN 1 86343 219 1

Distribution and Sales Enquiries
Australia: J.B. Fairfax Press Pty Limited
Tel: (02) 361 6366 Fax: (02) 360 6262
United Kingdom: J.B. Fairfax Press Limited
Tel: (01933) 402330 Fax: (01933) 402234